11/10 BVL

W9-BDL-712

Kentucky
The Bluegrass State

Jason Glaser

PowerKiDS press

New York

To all my siblings and siblings-in-law. May the sun shine bright on your homes as well.

Published in 2010 by The Rosen Publishing Group, Inc.
29 East 21st Street, New York, NY 10010

Copyright © 2010 by The Rosen Publishing Group, Inc.

All rights reserved. No part of this book may be reproduced in any form without permission in writing from the publisher, except by a reviewer.

First Edition

Editor: Amelie von Zumbusch
Book Design: Greg Tucker
Photo Researcher: Jessica Gerweck

Photo Credits: Cover © Bob Krist/Corbis; p. 5 © Jeff Greenberg/age fotostock; p. 7 MPI/Getty Images; pp. 9, 22 (tree, flag, bird, flower) Shutterstock.com; p. 11 © www.iStockphoto.com/Brian Swartz; p. 13 © Dennis MacDonald/age fotostock; p. 15 © Walter Bibikow/JAI/Corbis; p. 17 Andy Lyons/Getty Images; p. 19 © Tom Till/age fotostock; p. 22 (horse) ©www.iStockphoto.com/Justyna Furmanczyk; p. 22 (Abraham Lincoln) Alexander Gardner/Getty Images; p. 22 (Muhammad Ali) Focus on Sport/Getty Images; p. 22 (Johnny Depp) Jon Furniss/Wire Image/Getty Images.

Library of Congress Cataloging-in-Publication Data

Glaser, Jason.
  Kentucky : the Bluegrass State / Jason Glaser. — 1st ed.
      p. cm. — (Our amazing states)
  Includes index.
  ISBN 978-1-4358-9396-2 (library binding) — ISBN 978-1-4358-9784-7 (pbk.) — ISBN 978-1-4358-9785-4 (6-pack)
  1. Kentucky—Juvenile literature. I. Title.
  F451.3.G53 2010
  976.9—dc22
                                    2009030284

Manufactured in the United States of America

CPSIA Compliance Information: Batch #WW10PK: For Further Information contact Rosen Publishing, New York, New York at 1-800-237-9932

Contents

True Blue — 4

West from Virginia — 6

Land Shaped by Water — 8

Living Off the Land — 10

Only in Kentucky — 12

Choosing Frankfort — 14

A History of Horses — 16

Mammoth Cave National Park — 18

Beautiful Kentucky — 20

Glossary — 21

Kentucky at a Glance — 22

Index — 24

Web Sites — 24

True Blue

Kentucky bluegrass is a lot like the state of Kentucky itself. For one thing, bluegrass is not really blue, just as Kentucky is not officially called a state. Kentucky's official name is the **Commonwealth** of Kentucky. Bluegrass is not native to America. It came from England, as did many early Kentuckians. Today, bluegrass is among first things people picture when they think about Kentucky. A type of **folk music** played in Kentucky is even called bluegrass music.

Kentucky is circled by seven other states. West Virginia and Virginia are on the east side, and Missouri is on the western tip. Tennessee runs along Kentucky's south side while Illinois, Indiana, and Ohio sit across the Ohio River to the north.

Bluegrass music uses a number of instruments, including the banjo and the fiddle. The man here is holding a banjo, while the boy is learning to play the fiddle.

West from Virginia

By the 1700s, England ruled 13 colonies in eastern North America. The English wanted their colonies to grow, giving more land to England. Settlers headed west from the Virginia Colony and entered American Indian hunting grounds that became known as Kentucky.

In 1775, American colonists broke away from England, which started the American Revolution. The colonists won the war and kept moving west. Soon, Kentucky had enough people to become a new state. Kentucky became the fifteenth state in 1792. Its ties to Virginia remained strong, though. Even when Kentucky stayed with the **Union** during the **Civil War**, as many as 40,000 Kentuckians fought with Virginia and the Southern states.

Daniel Boone (center, in yellow) led many settlers to Kentucky. He used the Wilderness Road, which led through a break in the mountains called the Cumberland Gap.

Land Shaped by Water

Virginians entering Kentucky first had to pass through the Appalachian Mountains on Kentucky's east side. The Cumberland Gap, an open valley in the mountains, was the easiest way to reach the lands beyond. The Cumberland Gap was formed by river water.

Kentucky is covered in rivers. It has the most waterways of any state besides Alaska. Rivers form many of the state's borders. Other large rivers run across the central grassy hills and through the swampy southwest lowlands. In southeastern Kentucky, you can visit Cumberland Falls, a waterfall on the Cumberland River. It is one of the few places where you can see a moonbow, or nighttime rainbow.

Many visitors come to Cumberland Falls State Resort Park to view the falls, seen here. Visitors to the park can also go fishing, rafting, horseback riding, and hiking.

Living Off the Land

Early settlers ate their fill in Kentucky. Many kinds of animals the settlers hunted are still around, including deer, black bears, wild turkeys, and elk. Berry bushes, chestnut trees, and walnut trees grew there then and grow there today. Early settlers made drinks using the Kentucky coffee tree or a mint plant called pennyroyal. Today, people no longer use these plants. We now know that their leaves are poisonous if you have too much of them!

The state's best-known plant is likely Kentucky bluegrass, the state plant. As bluegrass grows, blue buds form on the plant's green stems. This sometimes gives bluegrass a bluish color. When tall bluegrass blows in the wind, Kentuckians say that a blue mist hangs over the field.

These horses are eating Kentucky bluegrass. Kentucky's rich bluegrass supplies food for both wild animals and farm animals.

Only in Kentucky

There are many special things that come from Kentucky. Louisville Slugger wooden baseball bats are made in Louisville, Kentucky. These bats are used by many of the top baseball players. Many of the finest racehorses in the world are raised in Kentucky. Kentucky also supplies almost all the world's bourbon, a kind of **alcohol**.

Kentuckians make lots of things that people around the country use every day. The state's farmers grow corn, rye, barley, wheat, and tobacco. Miners dig coal out of the earth. Workers build cars, trucks, buses, and other **vehicles**. At Appliance Park, in Louisville, workers build refrigerators, freezers, and washing machines.

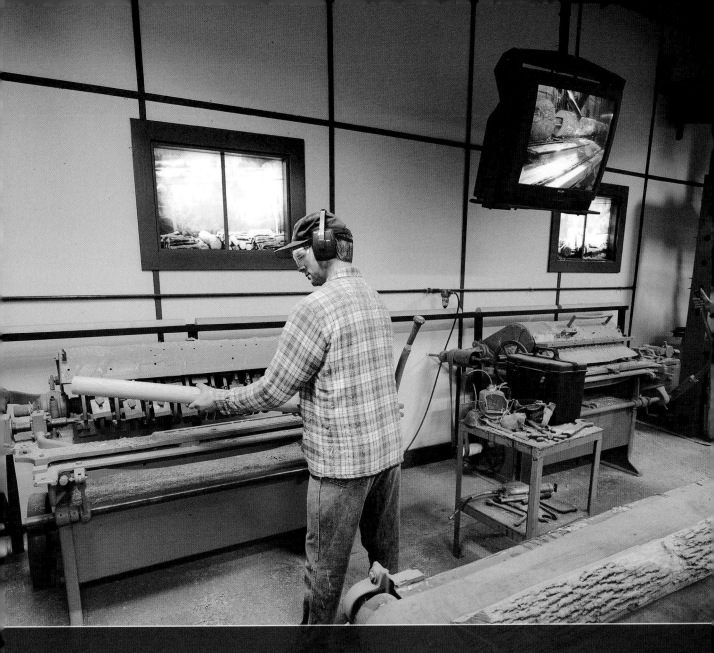

This worker is crafting a Louisville Slugger. Today, you can visit the Louisville Slugger Museum & Factory in downtown Louisville.

Choosing Frankfort

When it came time for Kentucky to choose a capital city, Frankfort was a natural choice. It was not the largest city, but a landowner there gave so much land and money for a capitol that state leaders could not say no! The capitol building borrows ideas from buildings around the world. It has a **dome** like that of the U.S. Capitol in Washington, D.C., and steps like those on the Opera House in Paris, France.

Frankfort is a good place to go to remember Daniel Boone. Boone was one of Kentucky's most famous people. He was also one of the first settlers in Kentucky. You can see pictures of Boone's exciting life on the capitol's walls. You can also visit a **gravestone** for him in the Frankfort Cemetery.

Kentucky's capitol, seen here, was built between 1904 and 1910. The state's lawmakers had decided that the old capitol, which had been built in 1830, was too small.

A History of Horses

Raising crops was likely the first business in Kentucky, but raising horses was close behind. Powerful racing horses called Thoroughbreds may have been raised in the state as early as 1779. Today, Thoroughbreds are Kentucky's state horse. People raise and train horses for racing and show jumping on the state's many horse farms. Horse lovers can learn about more than 50 kinds of horses at the Kentucky Horse Park, near Lexington, Kentucky.

The Kentucky Derby is known as the greatest 2 minutes in sports. This race, held on the first Saturday in May, has been fun for horse-racing fans since 1875. Every year people enjoy the race at Churchill Downs racetrack, in Louisville. They clap as the winning racehorse has roses placed around its neck.

The Kentucky Derby, seen here, is 1.25 miles (2 km) long. Special riders, called jockeys, ride the horses in this stirring race.

Mammoth Cave National Park

Much of the rock under Kentucky's rich soil is limestone. Rain and river water can wear away limestone. This creates large cave tunnels like those at Mammoth Cave National Park. "Mammoth" means "big." The cave is named well. Mammoth Cave is the world's largest underground cave!

Mammoth Cave draws thousands of visitors each year. If you bring along a flashlight when you visit, you can see how the rock has slowly formed pointed cones above your head. A guide might show you saltpeter, a **mineral** mined to make **gunpowder**. There are even animals with no eyes there since it is always dark. However, you will never see it all because Mammoth Cave is more than 365 miles (587 km) long!

Mammoth Cave National Park, seen here, is beautiful above ground, too. It is home to birds, frogs, fish, and more than 1,300 kinds of flowering plants.

Beautiful Kentucky

Some people say that Kentucky is as good as gold. Maybe that is because Kentucky holds the country's store of gold in the **depository** at Fort Knox. You could also say Kentucky is a work of art, like some of those from the Berea Craft Festival. Talented artists sell bedspreads, pots, **jewelry**, and more at this fair in Berea, Kentucky.

To many, the greatest work of art is Kentucky itself. From the shining streams and grassy hills to the golden leaves of fall, Kentucky has some of the most beautiful land in America. Kentuckians are also proud of the crafts, music, and foods that make Kentucky famous around the world. As their state song says, many Kentuckians love their "Old Kentucky Home."

Glossary

alcohol (AL-kuh-hol) A liquid, such as beer or wine, that can make a person lose control or get drunk.

Civil War (SIH-vul WOR) The war fought between the Northern and the Southern states of America from 1861 to 1865.

commonwealth (KAH-mun-welth) A nation or state founded on what is right for the common good.

depository (dih-PO-zuh-tawr-ee) A place where something is stored.

dome (DOHM) A type of curved roof.

folk music (FOHK MYOO-sik) Music that is handed down among people.

gravestone (GRAYV-stohn) A stone that marks where a dead person was buried.

gunpowder (GUN-pow-dur) A black powder that explodes in a gun and moves the bullet.

jewelry (JOO-ul-ree) Objects worn on the body that are made of special metals, such as gold and silver, and valued stones.

mineral (MIN-rul) A natural thing that is not an animal, a plant, or another living thing.

Union (YOON-yun) The Northern states that stayed with the national government during the Civil War.

vehicles (VEE-uh-kulz) Objects that move or carry things.

Kentucky State Symbols

State Tree
Tulip Poplar

State Horse
Thoroughbred

State Flag

State Bird
Cardinal

State Flower
Goldenrod

State Seal

Famous People from Kentucky

Abraham Lincoln
(1809–1865)
Born in Hardin County, KY
U.S. President

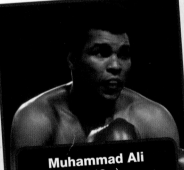
Muhammad Ali
(1942–)
Born in Louisville, KY
Boxer

Johnny Depp
(1963–)
Born in Owensboro, KY
Actor

Kentucky State Map

Legend

○ Major City

★ Capital

~ River

Kentucky State Facts

Population: About 4,041,769

Area: 40,395 square miles (104,623 sq km)

Motto: "United We Stand, Divided We Fall"

Song: "My Old Kentucky Home," words and music by Stephen Collins Foster

Index

A
American Revolution, 6
Appalachian Mountains, 8

B
bluegrass, 4, 10
Boone, Daniel, 14

C
Civil War, 6
Commonwealth of Kentucky, 4
Cumberland Gap, 8

E
England, 4, 6

F
folk music, 4

Fort Knox, 20

I
Illinois, 4
Indiana, 4

K
Kentucky Derby, 16

L
Lexington, Kentucky, 16
Louisville, Kentucky, 12, 16

M
Mammoth Cave National
    Park, 18
Mississippi Plateau, 8
Missouri, 4

O
Ohio, 4

S
settlers, 6, 10

T
Tennessee, 4
Thoroughbreds, 16

U
Union, 6

V
Virginia, 4, 6

W
West Virginia, 4

Web Sites

Due to the changing nature of Internet links, PowerKids Press has developed an online list of Web sites related to the subject of this book. This site is updated regularly. Please use this link to access the list:

www.powerkidslinks.com/amst/ky/